My First Picture Encyclopedia

Show Me
Community Helpers

by Clint Edwards

CAPSTONE PRESS
a capstone imprint

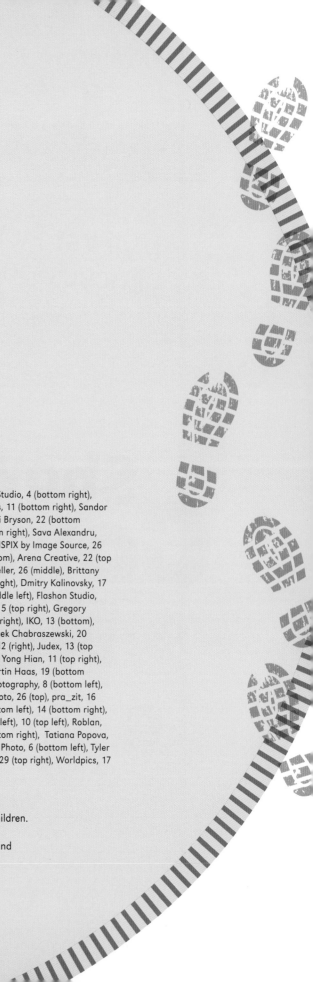

A+ Books are published by Capstone Press,
1710 Roe Crest Drive, North Mankato, Minnesota 56003.
www.capstonepub.com

Library of Congress Cataloging-in-Publication Data
Edwards, Clint.
Show me community helpers : my first picture encyclopedia / by Clint Edwards.
p. cm.—(A+ books)
Includes bibliographical references.
Summary: "Defines through text and photos core terms related to community helpers"—
Provided by publisher.
ISBN 978-1-62065-056-1 (library binding)
ISBN 978-1-62065-918-2 (paper over board)
ISBN 978-1-4765-1242-6 (ebook pdf)
1. Municipal services—Juvenile literature. 2. Professions—Juvenile literature.
3. Community life—Juvenile literature. 4. Communities—Juvenile literature. I. Title.
HD4431.E39 2013
331.7—dc23   2012033202

Editorial Credits
Aaron Sautter, editor; Bobbie Nuytten, designer; Svetlana Zhurkin, media researcher;
Laura Manthe, production specialist

Photo Credits
Capstone Press, 23 (top right); Capstone Studio: Karon Dubke, cover (bottom left); Dreamstime: Flashon Studio, 4 (bottom right),
Kurhan, cover (top right), 1 (top right), Mitja Mladkovic, 7 (top), 23 (bottom left), Monkey Business Images, 11 (bottom right), Sandor
Kacso, 16 (bottom left), Thomas Lammeyer, 9 (bottom right); iStockphotos: Baris Simsek, 21 (top left), Jani Bryson, 22 (bottom
right), Naheed Choudhry, 11 (top middle), Nancy Louie, 22 (top right), RiverNorthPhotography, 23 (bottom right), Sava Alexandru,
8 (top); Shutterstock: Adrian Chinery, 7 (middle), aerogondo2, 9 (bottom left), Africa Studio, 6 (top left), AISPIX by Image Source, 26
(bottom), Alexander Raths, 13 (top left), andersphoto, 16 (top right), Annette Shaff, 31 (top right and bottom), Arena Creative, 22 (top
left), Arkady Mazor, 27 (bottom), AVAVA, 20 (right), Baloncici, 28 (top right), Bambuh, 5 (middle), Bjorn Heller, 26 (middle), Brittany
Courville, 30 (bottom left), Chas, 14 (bottom left), Cosmin Manci, 18 (bottom), dcwcreations, 8 (bottom right), Dmitry Kalinovsky, 17
(bottom left), 28 (top left), 29 (top left and bottom right), Eric Isselée, 18 (top), Federico Rostagno, 27 (middle left), Flashon Studio,
21 (top right), 25 (bottom right), 30 (top right), Frances A. Miller, 29 (bottom left), Gelpi, 12 (left), Gorgev, 5 (top right), Gregory
James Van Raalte, 4 (top), Gunnar Pippel, 7 (bottom right), hightowernrw, 17 (top right), hxdbzxy, 25 (top right), IKO, 13 (bottom),
Ioannis Ioannou, 11 (bottom left), iofoto, back cover (bottom middle), 7 (bottom left), 20 (bottom left), Jacek Chabraszewski, 20
(top left), James Steidl, 5 (top left), Jaren Jai Wicklund, 21 (bottom left), Jerry Sharp, 9 (top right), jgl247, 12 (right), Judex, 13 (top
middle), Kostia, 19 (bottom right), Kurhan, 5 (bottom), 25 (bottom left), Le Do, cover (bottom middle), Lim Yong Hian, 11 (top right),
LongQuattro (footprints), cover, back cover, 1, 2, Lucky Business, 22 (bottom left), majeczka, 27 (top), Martin Haas, 19 (bottom
left), Michael C. Gray, 13 (top right), Monkey Business Images, 13 (middle), 25 (top left), Morgan Lane Photography, 8 (bottom left),
nfsphoto, 16 (bottom right), Odua Images (torn paper), cover, 1, Oleg Kharkhan, 27 (middle right), perlphoto, 26 (top), pra_zit, 16
(top left), Renewer, 10 (bottom right), Richard Thornton, 31 (top left), Rob Byron, back cover (top), 10 (bottom left), 14 (bottom right),
15 (top left), Rob Marmion, 14 (top), 23 (top left), Rob Wilson, back cover (middle and bottom left), 9 (top left), 10 (top left), Roblan,
14 (bottom middle), shock, 15 (bottom), sima, 17 (bottom right), Sonya Etchison, 24 (top), sydeen, 30 (bottom right), Tatiana Popova,
30 (top left), Tommaso79, 6 (top right), Travis Klein, 24 (bottom), trekandshoot, 6 (bottom right), Trinacria Photo, 6 (bottom left), Tyler
Hartl, 4 (bottom left), Tyler Olson, cover (bottom right), 10 (top right), 11 (top left), 19 (top), warren0909, 29 (top right), Worldpics, 17
(top left), XPhantom, 28 (bottom); Svetlana Zhurkin, 15 (top right), 21 (bottom right)

Note to Parents, Teachers, and Librarians
My First Picture Encyclopedias provide an early introduction to reference materials for young children.
These accessible, visual encyclopedias support literacy development by building subject-specific
vocabularies and research skills. Stimulating format, inviting content, and phonetic aids assist and
encourage young readers.

Printed in the United States of America in North Mankato, Minnesota.

092012   006933CGS13

Table of Contents

Get to Know Community Helpers

Community helpers are found all around us. They work in hospitals to keep people safe and healthy. They work in schools and libraries to help people learn new things. They grow food and fix things to help serve people's daily needs. Community helpers work to help others every day.

emergency helpers

workers who help keep people safe from harm; police officers, firefighters, and EMTs are emergency helpers

community

a group of people who live in the same place; it could be a city, town, or neighborhood

911

a telephone number people should call for help in an emergency

medical helpers

workers who help keep people healthy; doctors, nurses, and dentists are medical helpers

education helpers

workers who help people learn; teachers, teacher assistants, and librarians are education helpers

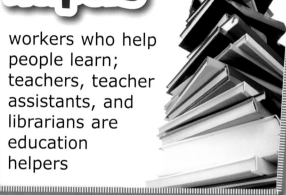

daily helpers

workers who help meet people's daily needs; farmers, construction workers, and electric utility workers are daily helpers

Keeping People Safe

Police Officers

Police officers keep people safe. They make sure people obey the law. Police officers study crime scenes, arrest people who commit crimes, and enforce traffic laws.

fingerprint

the unique pattern made by the curved ridges on the tips of a person's fingers; police officers use fingerprints to identify people

crime

an action that breaks the law

holster

a holder for a police officer's handgun

jail

a place where criminals are held

6

police car

a specially equipped car with radios, cameras, computers, sirens, and lights; some police officers don't use cars; they travel by bicycle, motorcycle, or horse

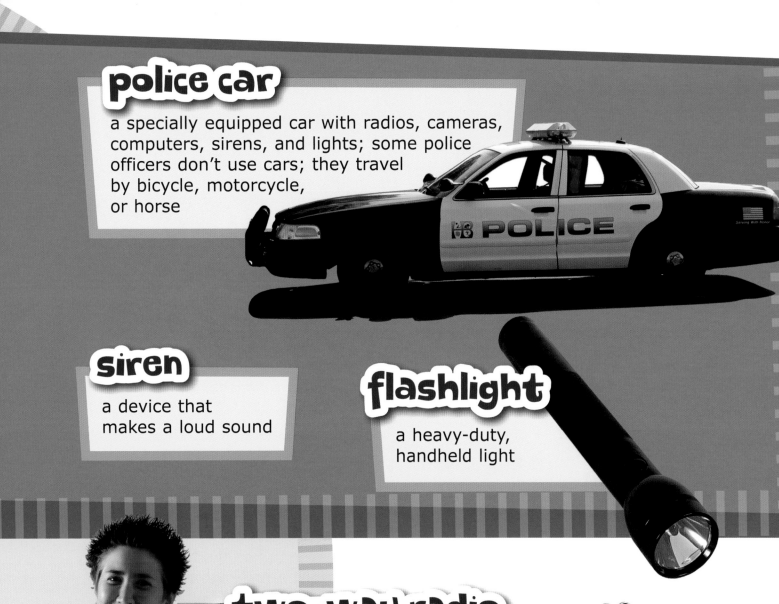

siren

a device that makes a loud sound

flashlight

a heavy-duty, handheld light

two-way radio

a radio used to communicate with another radio on the same channel

badge

a small metal shield with symbols and information about where a police officer works

handcuffs

metal rings joined by a chain that are locked around a prisoner's wrists to prevent escape

Firefighters

Firefighters work to protect people, homes, and businesses when a fire breaks out. Firefighters also teach people about fire safety.

fire station

a building that houses fire trucks, firefighting equipment, and firefighters

fire engine

a vehicle used to carry fire hoses and other equipment; fire engines also pump water from a fire hydrant through hoses to help put out fires

fire hydrant

an upright pipe with a spout or nozzle that supplies water for fighting fires; fire hydrants are connected to large pipes called water mains

fire extinguisher

a metal container used to spray chemicals on fires to help put them out

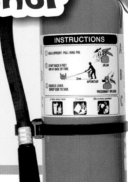

ladder truck

a truck with a long ladder used to reach the tops of buildings

air tank

a tank that holds air; firefighters carry air tanks to help them breath in smoke-filled buildings

helmet

a hard hat that protects the head

fireproof clothing

specially treated clothing that does not easily catch fire

ax

a tool with a sharp blade on the end of a handle

fire hose

a large hose used to spray water on flames

Emergency Medical Technicians

Emergency medical technicians (EMTs) are trained to treat patients at accident scenes and in ambulances. They respond to 911 calls, perform CPR, and treat serious wounds.

team

a group of people who work together; EMTs work in teams of two people

ambulance

a vehicle used to take sick or injured people to a hospital; an ambulance has sirens, flashing lights, and a loud horn

defibrillator

(de-FIB-rih-lay-tor) a medical tool used to start a person's heart

medical helicopter

a helicopter used to fly sick or injured people to a hospital; sometimes a helicopter is sent where an ambulance cannot reach

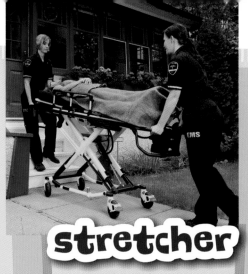

splint

a piece of wood, plastic, or metal used to support a broken bone

stretcher

a bed with straps and wheels used to move patients

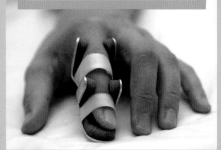

IV bag

a plastic bag used to quickly give fluids, nutrients, or medicine to patients; IV bags usually hang from a pole

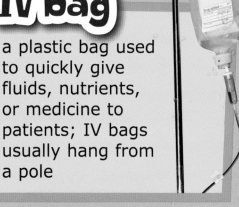

CPR

a treatment used to help a patient whose heart has stopped beating; CPR involves pressing on a patient's chest in a certain rhythm and breathing into his or her mouth

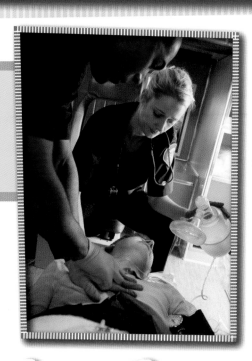

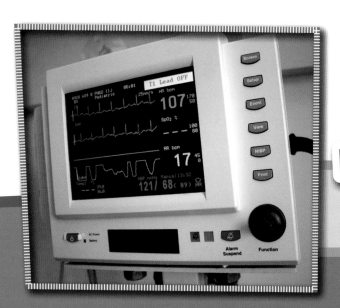

heart monitor

an electronic device that tracks a patient's heartbeat

Keeping People Healthy

Doctors help people who are sick or hurt. They treat wounds, perform surgeries, and give medicine to help sick people feel better.

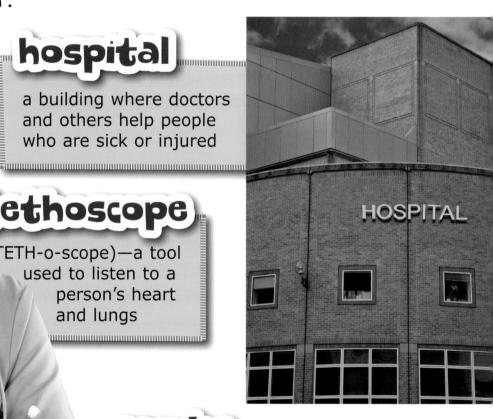

hospital
a building where doctors and others help people who are sick or injured

stethoscope
(STETH-o-scope)—a tool used to listen to a person's heart and lungs

scrubs
protective clothing worn by doctors, nurses, and others in an operating room

HOSPITAL

otoscope

(OH-tuh-scope)—a tool used to look inside a person's ears

ophthalmoscope

(op-THUHL-muh-skope)—a tool used to examine a person's eyes

scalpel

(SKAL-puhl)—a small, sharp medical knife

patient

a person who receives medical care

tongue depressor

a tool that looks like a popsicle stick; it keeps the tongue out of the way so a doctor or nurse can look at a patient's throat

stitches

a medical treatment using a needle and thread to close a wound

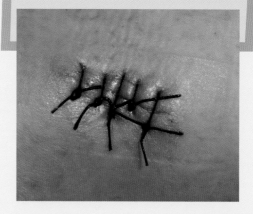

Nurses

Nurses help keep people healthy. They help sick people get well. Some nurses work with doctors in operating rooms. Nurse practitioners give people checkups.

checkup

a regular medical exam to check a person's overall health

vital signs

signs of life that nurses check; pulse rate, temperature, breathing, and blood pressure are vital signs

pulse

a steady beat or throb felt as the heart moves blood through the body

blood pressure cuff

a tool used to check a patient's blood pressure

thermometer

a tool used to measure a person's body temperature

needle and syringe

(suh-RINJ)—tools used to give a patient a shot of medicine

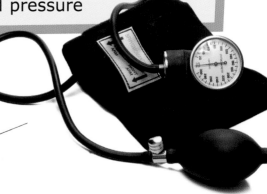

Pharmacists

A pharmacist studies, prepares, and sells medicine. Pharmacists work with doctors to give people medicine needed to get well. They tell people how to safely use medicine.

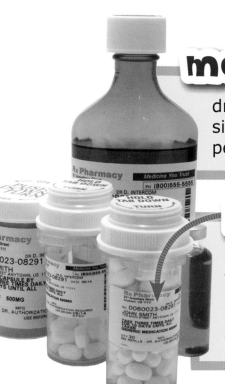

medicine
drugs used to help sick or injured people get better

label
directions attached to pill bottles that tell patients how much medicine to take and when to take it

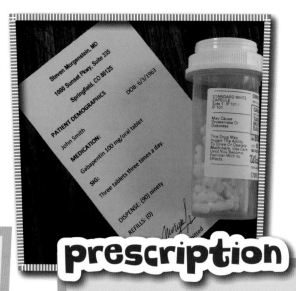

prescription
(pri-SKRIP-shuhn) an order for medicine from a doctor, dentist, or nurse practitioner

pharmacy
(FAR-muh-see) a store where medicine is sold; pharmacies can be found in hospitals, grocery stores, shopping centers, and on the Internet

Dentists and Hygienists

Dentists and hygienists take care of people's teeth. They show them how to brush and floss. Hygienists clean teeth. Dentists fix people's teeth by filling cavities.

dental drill

a small, high-speed drill used to clean and prepare cavities to be filled

X-ray

a picture of a person's teeth used to find cavities

cavity

a hole in a tooth that is caused by decay; dentists fill cavities with a special material

fluoride

(FLOOR-eyed)—a mineral dentists apply to teeth to help prevent cavities; fluoride is often added to drinking water and toothpaste

plaque

(PLAK)—a sticky substance that can build up on a person's teeth; plaque contains germs that cause tooth decay and gum disease

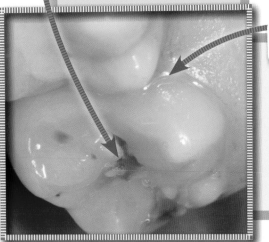

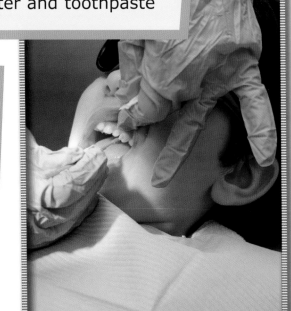

mouth mirror

a small mirror used to see inside a patient's mouth

floss

special string used to clean between teeth

dental hook

a small tool with a hook used to scrape away plaque

saliva ejector

a suction tube used to remove saliva and other fluids from a patient's mouth

polisher

a tool with a rotating tip used to clean teeth

air-water syringe

a metal tool that sprays water or air to clean and dry a patient's teeth

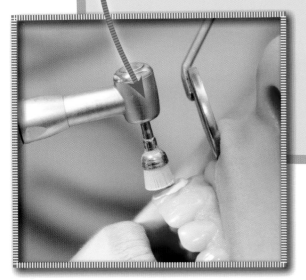

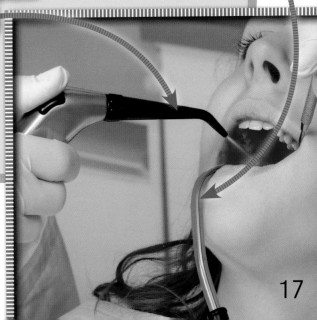

Veterinarians

Veterinarians (vet-ur-uh-NAYR-ee-uhns) are doctors who take care of animals. They treat sick or injured pets. They take care of horses, cows, and other farm animals. Vets help keep animals healthy and happy.

vaccination

(vak-suh-NAY-shun) medicine that protects people and pets from disease

parasite

(PAIR-uh-site)—an animal that lives on or in another animal to get nourishment; fleas, ticks, and worms are common parasites; vets give medicine to remove parasites from pets

18

sterilize

to remove an animal's ability to reproduce; pets are often sterilized to prevent unwanted offspring and some illnesses

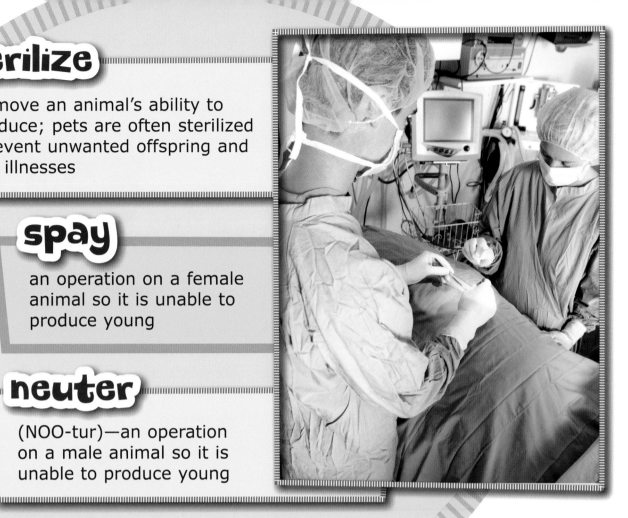

spay

an operation on a female animal so it is unable to produce young

neuter

(NOO-tur)—an operation on a male animal so it is unable to produce young

scale

a tool used to weigh something; veterinarians use special scales designed to weigh animals

neck cone

a cone worn around an animal's neck to keep it from licking or biting its wounds; cones do not hurt

Helping People Learn

Teachers

Teachers help students learn to read, write, do math, and speak other languages. They prepare lessons, assign and grade homework, and test students to see how much they are learning.

curriculum

a plan for what students should study

homework

school assignments that students do after school, usually at home

test

a quiz or exam used to find out how well students are learning

lesson plan

ideas about how to teach skills and share information

grade

the score a teacher gives a student's work

interactive whiteboard

a large board connected to a computer and projector; teachers use these boards to help teach lessons to students

flash cards

cards that have words or math problems on one side and answers on the other; they are used as learning aids

field trip

a visit to a place to see and learn new things

principal

the person who runs a school

Librarians

Librarians organize books, magazines, and other materials at libraries. They help people find information from many places. They also plan story time and other activities.

scanner

a laser device used to check books and materials in and out of a library

library

a place where books, magazines, and other items are kept for reading, reference, and lending

story time

a time when a librarian reads a story out loud

audio book

a recording of someone reading a book out loud

Internet

a system that connects computers all over the world; librarians help people use the Internet on library computers

Dewey Decimal System

a numbering system librarians use to organize books based on their subjects

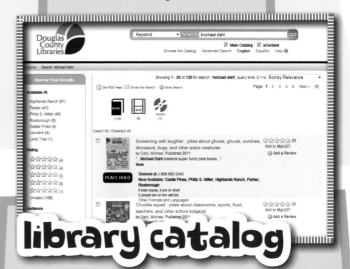

library catalog

a list of a library's books and materials; lists usually include titles, authors, subjects, call numbers, and the years published or released

e-reader

an electronic device used to read digital books

bookmobile

a large vehicle used as a traveling library

School Bus Drivers

School bus drivers drive students to school. They make sure students follow bus rules. They keep students safe by stopping traffic and following traffic laws.

bus stop
a place where people wait for a bus and are dropped off

school bus
a large yellow vehicle that transports students to and from school; flashing lights on a bus warn other drivers to watch carefully for students getting on or off the bus

passenger
someone besides the driver who rides in a vehicle

stop sign
a red sign attached to a bus with "STOP" printed in the middle; buses use stop signs to stop traffic while picking up and dropping off students

emergency exit
a door that is used to get off the bus only in an emergency

Cafeteria Workers

hairnet

light netting worn over a person's hair to keep it in place; hairnets keep hair from falling into food

School cafeteria workers prepare and serve healthy meals for students. School custodians clean school buildings. They make sure everything is in working order.

cafeteria

a dining area where meals are served and eaten

cooking apron

a long piece of fabric worn to protect clothing

Custodians

vacuum cleaner

mop

a handheld tool used for scrubbing floors

an electric tool used to clean dirt from carpets and other surfaces

Serving People's Needs

Farmers

Farmers grow plants and raise animals. They produce much of the food we eat. There are livestock farmers, crop farmers, dairy farmers, and poultry farmers.

farm
an area of land used for growing crops and raising animals

tractor
a powerful vehicle used to pull and power farm machines

barn
a farm building used to store crops and equipment; barns also provide shelter for farm animals

crops
plants that produce food, such as corn, wheat, and soybeans

combine
a large machine used to harvest crops

livestock

farm animals such as cows, horses, sheep, and pigs

poultry

birds, such as chickens or turkeys, raised on farms for their eggs or meat

irrigation

(ihr-uh-GAY-shuhn) a way to supply water to crops using a system of pipes or channels

dairy farm

a farm where cows are raised for their milk

Construction Workers

Construction workers build houses, schools, shopping centers, and more. They use small tools and big machines to construct large buildings.

backhoe
a digging machine that has a bucket at the end of a long arm

crane
a machine with a long arm used to lift and move heavy objects

construction site
a place where workers build a building

bulldozer
a powerful machine with a wide blade or large bucket at the front; bulldozers move earth, rocks, and rubble

concrete

a mixture of cement, water, sand, and gravel that hardens when it dries

drill

a power tool with an attachment that spins quickly to make holes in wood and other materials

hard hat

a hat made from hard plastic, worn to protect a worker's head

safety harness

a belt and straps worn to keep a worker from falling from high places

safety glasses

shatter-proof glasses worn to protect a worker's eyes

gloves

coverings that protect a worker's hands

Electric Utility Workers

Electric utility workers make sure electricity flows to people's homes and businesses. Sometimes big storms knock down power lines. Workers use special equipment to repair the lines.

electricity

a natural force that can be used to make light and heat or to make machines work

lift truck

a large truck with a long arm and an attached bucket; used to lift workers up to high power lines

power plant

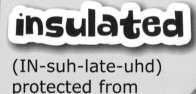

a building or group of buildings used to create electricity

insulated

(IN-suh-late-uhd) protected from electric shock by materials that block the flow of electricity

digger derrick

a large truck with an attached crane and post-hole digger; used to install power poles

pole-climbing gaffs

metal hooks with a spike used by utility workers to climb power poles

power line

a cable made from copper or aluminum that carries electricity from power plants to homes and businesses

high-voltage

electricity that is powerful enough to cause injury or death

hot stick

an insulated pole made of fiberglass; used for safely working with live power lines

Read More

Kalman, Bobbie. *Helpers in My Community.* My World. New York: Crabtree Pub. Company, 2010.

Tourville, Amanda Doering. *Whose Equipment is This?* Community Helper Mysteries. Mankato, Minn.: Capstone Press, 2012.

Wohlrabe, Sarah C. *A Visit to the Library.* My Community. Mankato, Minn.: Capstone Press, 2011.

Titles in this set:

Show me
COMMUNITY HELPERS

Show me
POLAR ANIMALS

Show me
DINOSAURS

Show me
REPTILES

Show me
DOGS

Show me
SPACE

Show me
INSECTS

Show me
TRANSPORTATION

Internet Sites

FactHound offers a safe, fun way to find Internet sites related to this book. All of the sites on FactHound have been researched by our staff.

Here's all you do:

Visit *www.facthound.com*

Type in this code: 9781620650561

Super-cool stuff!

Check out projects, games and lots more at
www.capstonekids.com